A Life of Significance with Jesus

SERIES

Finding a
Place to Serve

wesleyan
publishing
house

Indianapolis, Indiana

Copyright © 2007 by Wesleyan Publishing House
Published by Wesleyan Publishing House
Indianapolis, Indiana 46250
Printed in the United States of America

ISBN: 978-0-89827-371-7

Written by Anita Eastlack.

Cover design by Kory Pence.

D-SERIES

A Life of Significance with Jesus

Everyone wants their life to count for something significant. People everywhere are spending their lives for fading artifacts and fleeting glory. Significance, value, legacy, and impact are the desired outcome of every investment. The desire of believers in Jesus Christ should be no different. Those who are true followers of Jesus Christ are to be interested in becoming more and more like Him. Following Jesus and getting closer to Him *IS* significance, value, legacy, and impact for a Christian.

The *D Series* works by connecting every person to a solid relationship with Jesus. The scope of what we can learn and live for Jesus is limitless. But this series will get every believer on the right path—no matter where your starting point is. Regardless if you are a new believer or a seasoned disciple, this series is filled with truth for every person in the local Church.

What is significant about the *D Series* is the expectation that participants will actually live what they are studying. It is not enough to fill our heads and hearts with Jesus. We must follow through and make sure His love and interest in others show up in our service and daily activity. In other words, Christlike, holy living results when we use our heads, hearts, hands, and habits to focus on and represent Jesus.

Give yourself, your time, and your focus to Jesus through the *D Series*. Live your beliefs out in Jesus everyday!

THE COMMUNITY OF
SPIRITUAL FORMATION

To illustrate it simply, there are four areas to engage: the head, heart, hands, and habits. Start by seeking knowledge and understanding of Jesus Christ. This wisdom will enter your heart and miraculously transform it. A unified heart and mind leads to a wholehearted expression of love through compassionate service. This outpouring of compassion becomes a daily way of life where we are given daily grace by God's Holy Spirit to live a holy life.

Coming full circle—your growing wisdom, unified heart, compassionate service, and daily holy living—you are driven to a community of spiritual formation where every believer looks more and more like Jesus. The result is a solid relationship with Jesus and a lasting significance, value, legacy, and impact in the lives of those we serve.

Dr. Jim Dunn
General Director
Spiritual Formation Department
The Wesleyan Church

Community of Spiritual Formation
Discipleship to look more like Jesus.

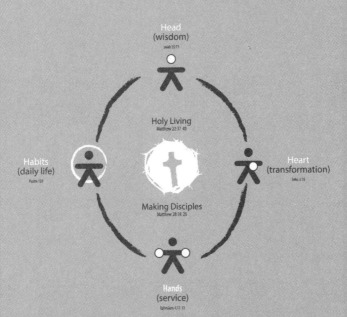

Contents

Introduction

Going to a funeral is one of the best ways to get perspective. In fact, a Christian memorial service is inspiring. Why? Funerals remind us of the facts of life: Life is short; life is about people not things; life is about character and giving of oneself; life is meaningful only when we leave a meaningful legacy behind. Do you yearn for fulfillment? Give. Serve.

Service is a prominent theme in our contemporary culture. September 11, 2001, awoke us to a renewed priority of caring for humanity. That awful day was like one big funeral. Our nation came face to face with her mortality. And, soon after that infamous day came devastating hurricanes, tsunamis, war, earthquakes, and massacres. We also opened our eyes to the disturbing plight of countless sex-trafficking and HIV/AIDS victims across the world.

Many have answered the call: American schools adopted Afghan schools; entrepreneurial children are funding projects; Micro businesses are changing the way of life in remote parts of the planet. Even Hollywood has found a constructive way to use their millions!

As Christians we have a special responsibility and reason to serve. We bring the hope of Jesus along with care. Let's not be followers. Let's lead the way. We do not need to change our beliefs to do this, especially as Wesleyans; we just need to be who we are!

We Were Created to Serve

PHILLIPPIANS 2:5-11

INTRODUCTION

God created us to serve, and Jesus is our example.

Before He was crucified, Jesus showed the disciples "the full extent of his love" (John 13:1). The King of Kings became a servant.

He washed their feet.

Peter protested. Jesus insisted.

Jesus finished this lesson with, "Do you understand what I have done for you? . . . you also should wash one another's feet. I have set you an example that you should do as I have done for you . . . Now that you know these things, you will be blessed if you do them" (John 13:12, 14–15, 17).

Today you'll explore why you were created—to serve.

ICEBREAKER

Reflect back on some of the times when you gave of yourself and found that it brought you joy and fulfillment.

Share with your group if there were any times when you did not initially want to serve, but after you did, you wanted to go back again (i.e. visit a nursing home, soup kitchen).

Tell of a time when someone served you in a meaningful way. List some of the effects the experience had on you.

DISCOVERING TRUTH—HEAD

We are all born with a selfish nature. We want others to accommodate us and serve our needs and desires. It begins all so innocently when we are helpless babies *needing* someone else to meet our every need and desire. However, as we grow we also need to mature, because we are also born with the innate need to be fulfilled. When we refuse to mature, our immaturity breeds selfishness. Selfishness never brings fulfillment. We need meaning in life. We need purpose. Jesus is our ultimate example for life. He was born a baby, needing His parents to care for Him just as our parents cared for us. Of course, He grew older and started His ministry at age thirty. Not only in His teachings, but also in His example, Jesus demonstrated how to put aside personal rights and embrace a servant attitude, fulfilling His purpose.

Have someone in your group read aloud Philippians 2:5–8 slowly, pausing after each verse to provide time for reflection.

As you consider the reality of this passage, talk about all that Jesus had in heaven. Make a list of the heavenly rights and privileges that Jesus gave up to come to earth. In the light of this list, talk about the implications of maturity versus selfishness. Make a contrasting list of the

WE WERE CREATED TO SERVE

conditions that He lived with on earth. Again, talk about the implications of maturity versus selfishness that Jesus had to withstand and embrace living on earth amongst such imperfection.

How would the sacrifice of giving up heavenly comforts help Him to ultimately sacrifice His life on the cross?

In verse 8, it says that Jesus, "became obedient to death—even death on a cross!" In the context of this verse, how would you define "obedient"?

Share about a person in your life you have observed as having Jesus' servant attitude.

Jesus not only came to serve, He came out of His unconditional and undying love for us. Love is what motivated Him to come to earth. When we truly take in His love for us, we also will be motivated to serve.

Read Ephesians 5:1 in a couple different translations. If you do not have more than one translation, paraphrase it in your own words.

Have each person choose one word from the verse and give a synonym for that word. Now read the verse again, inserting each person's new word. Take time to talk about how this helps to make the verse come to life.

Our dignity comes from within. Anyone who has seen the well-ordered life of a true saint knows the dignity and the power such people possess. "Why you?" asked the incredulous disciple of Saint Francis. "Why is the whole world running after you?" The good saint replied that it was only because God could not find anyone more ordinary to bless. The world, then, does not always look for clever, intelligent people; neither is the best leader the one who is most prepared. Instead, it is the one whom God has exalted, who uses a towel rather than a scepter to reign.

—Steve DeNeff, *More Than Forgiveness*

EMBRACING TRUTH—HEART

Customer service is a high priority in the business world. Employers insist on "putting the customer first" because it ultimately motivates customers to fork over their money. When we serve others, we may find ourselves expecting them to thank us and even return the favor. Serving in Christ's name means that our motive is to glorify God rather than to get something in return.

Again, Jesus is our example. In putting "the customer first," He died so that all people may have life. He did not put a condition on His actions but, as Romans 5:8 says, "While we were still sinners, Christ died for us." Of course, His desire was that good would come out of His sacrifice. But He left the results up to God and us.

Have someone in your group read aloud Philippians 2:9–11. If someone has a different translation, read it aloud again for added impact. If you do not have another translation, paraphrase it on your own as a group, one verse at a time. What one word describes your feelings as you take in the truth of this passage?

Explore the results of Jesus' death on the cross in these verses. Write how this affects your motive for serving.

CONNECTING—HANDS

In John 3:16 it says that God loved the world so much that He gave. Love is behind all God does. In the same way, we need to put love into action.

Read 1 John 3:18 silently. If you wish, underline the verse, and in the margin, write, "Love is a verb." Also, write in the margin, "See 1 John 4:16." Read 1 John 4:16, and write in the margin, "Love is a noun. See 1 John 3:18."

Discuss how you can put both the noun and verb parts of love into practice.

As a way of demonstrating the "connecting hands" of this session, hold hands and ask a volunteer to pray for each member of the group to be able to live out the noun and verb part of love.

TAKE HOME—HABITS

What point today hit home the most to you during this session? Was it the fact that Jesus is our example? We serve without strings attached? Love needs to be our motivation? Love is action not theory? Choose one point that you would like the Holy Spirit to help you grow in. Partner with another person in your group and pray that God will enable each of you to make this change. Then commit to pray for each other every day this week.

Share with the group two people whom you are going to serve this coming week. Be as specific as you can, and make one of your choices a family member.

LOOKING FORWARD

The radio, TV, and newspapers make us aware of a great amount of bad news on a daily basis. Come next week prepared to tell and hear of the many wonderful things being done around the world in the name of Jesus. (Go online to find information about agencies and organizations involved in compassion ministries. Bring your findings to the meeting.)

DIG DEEPER

1. Read Philippians 2:5-11 in *The Message* or another modern translation. Take time to journal additional thoughts that reinforce today's lesson. What did you learn? Were you convicted of something? If so, write those thoughts in your journal. What action or decision do you want to make in your life as a result of what you learned?

2. Read chapters 3 and 4 in 1 John. Take note of the many times "love" is addressed. In fact, count the number of times the word *love* is used and write the number in the margin of your Bible as a reminder of its importance.

3. Look up the word *love* in your Bible's concordance or using a Bible search tool such as www.gospelcom.net. Read a variety of the verses, both from the Old and New Testaments. Summarize what you have learned in your journal. Share that learning with a friend.

DISCOVERING TRUTH - HEAD

Let the initial sacrifice of Jesus' leaving heaven further impact you by looking up and studying the Scriptures about heaven. Consider the initial sacrifices a person needs to make to have Jesus' attitude even before taking the first step to serve others. Pick out one attitude you will begin to put into practice.

Find a copy of Oswald Chambers' *My Utmost for His Highest*. Look up the topic "service" in the index, and read those entries.

OPTIONAL LEARNING ACTIVITY 2:

EMBRACING TRUTH - HEART

Encourage each person to journal serving experiences through the week. Be sure to follow through by serving the people that were mentioned during the group session. Include facts and feelings in the journal, and finish each entry with a prayer.

OPTIONAL LEARNING ACTIVITY 3:
CONNECTING - HANDS

Before you go out and serve the people in your life, it may be helpful to humbly begin with the people in your group. Pour some water in a basin, and wash each other's feet. The leader can prayerfully consider the logistics to decrease awkwardness and enhance meaning.

OPTIONAL LEARNING ACTIVITY 4:
CONNECTING - HANDS

As a group, choose a project to support for the duration of the study on serving. Collect money each time you meet, and pray for the people the project will support. Send the donation after you complete the study. For ideas, talk with your pastor, or look on Web sites such as worldhope.net.

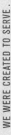

NOTES:
HEAD, HEART, HANDS & HABITS

God's Good News
All Around the World

MATTHEW 25:31-40

INTRODUCTION

Her daughter's hermit crab was a creepy pet, but less hassle than a dog! Caitlyn loved her little critter, Rainbow.

Then came the day to go away to camp. Caitlyn surprisingly cried during the good-bye. It was difficult for Anna too—perhaps it would be for any parent.

Sullen, Anna walked upstairs to the bedroom.

Of course—Rainbow! The cage sat on the dresser—with a note: "*Dear Mama, please feed Rainbow every day. Love, Caitlyn.*" Instantly, a love washed over Anna. Love for a crab? Yes! Not because it was a crab, but because it was Caitlyn's. If Caitlyn loved Rainbow, then she would too—until her daughter came home.

Jesus asks us to care for the "least of these" until He comes home. Will you?

ICEBREAKER

What kind of people do you find to be the hardest to love? Why?

List some of the people who seem to be the neediest.

There is so much bad news that we hear and read about every day. Share some of the good news you are aware of.

DISCOVERING TRUTH—HEAD

Sometimes evangelical Christians dismiss the importance of works, because we understand the truth of the Bible in that we are saved by grace. However, Jesus not only did not dismiss good deeds but gave them great importance. In Matthew 25 He told some very serious and sobering parables to warn us against being lazy in our faith. The first one shared the importance of being ready for Christ's return. The second showed the importance of using our talents rather than wasting them. The third parable is our text.

Have four volunteers stand and read Matthew 25:31–40 like a play. You will need a narrator, sheep, goats, and a king. Read with expression! Afterward, each person can take a turn to share his or her perceptions while role playing the particular part. What were your perceptions about the others in the parable?

List the good deeds the King named. Make a contemporary-equivalent list.

As a gesture of authenticity, go around the circle and answer the question, "If I were standing before the King at this moment, I would be a _____ (sheep or a goat).

> Service is the overflow of superabounding devotion; but, profoundly speaking, there is no call to that, it is my own little actual bit and is the echo of my identification with the nature of God. Service is the natural part of my life. God gets me into a relationship with Himself whereby I understand His call, then I do things out of sheer love for Him on my own account. To serve God is the deliberate love-gift of a nature that has heard the call of God.
>
> —Oswald Chambers, *My Utmost for His Highest*

Sometimes it is helpful to read Scripture in context. Go back to chapter 24 and the beginning of chapter 25. Read the headings of each section. How do all these teachings relate to each other?

The very first sentence in the book *The Purpose Driven Life* by Rick Warren reads, "It's not about you." Warren goes on to say, "The purpose of your life is far greater than your own personal fulfillment, your peace of mind, or even your happiness. It's far greater than your family, your career, or even your wildest dreams and ambitions. It you want to know why you were placed on this planet, you must begin with God. You were born *by* his purpose and *for* his purpose." If we are going to begin with God, then we need to go to His Word, the Bible.

Have everyone in the group close their eyes while a volunteer slowly reads Ephesians 2:10. While you are listening, take every word personally. How does this verse help to keep life about God rather than about us?

Read verses 4–9. How does this passage provide deeper emphasis to the points already made in the lesson?

EMBRACING TRUTH—HEART

Jesus takes our actions toward others personally. God's truth is this: How we treat others is how we are treating God. Have someone in your group look up and read

> You were put on earth to make a contribution. You weren't created to just consume resources—to eat, breathe, and take up space. God designed you to make a difference with your life. —Rick Warren, *The Purpose Driven Life*

Ephesians 6:7 and Matthew 10:42. Take some time to paraphrase these two verses.

Why is it so humanly hard to love God by loving people? What are some of the common barriers to loving people? Explore some ways to overcome those barriers. Divide into groups of two or three. Role play (overacting may be fun as well as driving the point home) some of the reactions that people have that display something other than loving others. For example, have someone role play an individual who needs to be loved and the others in the group react to that person in a typical manner.

What are some of your personal/human feelings that conflict with God's truth? Does it bother you that you have a conflict with God? If so, how? If not, explain.

Have a time of prayer as a group. Whether silently or aloud, encourage each person to confess God's truth and confess the need for God's help to live the truth.

Together, read John 8:32. Describe the results of being set free with God's truth. How will your heart be lighter and librated?

CONNECTING—HANDS

Love is a verb. First John 3:18 instructs us by saying, "Dear children, let us not love with words or tongue but with actions and in truth."

Make a mental list of the people with whom you interacted today. Begin with your family or those you encounter first in the morning. Consider your colleagues at work or at school, and those you encountered while traveling. With whom did you put love into action today? Is there anyone with whom you might need to make restitution or apologize to? When and how will you do that?

TAKE HOME—HABITS

Read the following poem aloud in unison:

Sow a thought, and you reap an act; / Sow an act, and you reap a habit; / Sow a habit, and you reap a character; / Sow a character, and you reap a destiny (Charles Reader).

GOD'S GOOD NEWS ALL AROUND THE WORLD

What is one important thought that you are willing to commit to keeping with you through this week that can affect your habit of serving others? Role play some possible scenarios that will offer opportunity to put this lesson into practice.

LOOKING FORWARD

Are you concerned or overwhelmed with this additional "have to" for your "to-do" list? Don't worry. Serving is a joy not a burden, and God has already given you the talents and skills you need to do what He wants you to do. We'll explore those gifts in the next session.

DIG DEEPER

1. Reflect on Proverbs 28:27 and Proverbs 31:8–9. Journal your thoughts and what you sense God is telling you personally through His Word.

2. Using a concordance or a Bible search tool such as www.gospelcom.net, examine several Bible passages that mention the word *serve* or *give*. Summarize what you have learned in a paragraph, and then share your paragraph with one of the members of your group.

3. The third chapter of Colossians gives instructions for relationships but can be quite controversial. Read the chapter, giving greatest attention to verses 17, 23, and 24. How can putting the emphasis on these three verses make a difference in your relationships?

DISCOVERING TRUTH – HEAD

Divide into two subgroups. Read and analyze Matthew 20:20–28, making note of the requests and reactions of all the people involved. Gather together as one group and share your findings. Conclude with each one identifying the person he or she most relates to in the passage.

OPTIONAL LEARNING ACTIVITY 2:

EMBRACING TRUTH – HEART

Read Purpose 4 (days 29–35) in *The Purpose Driven Life* by Rick Warren.

CONNECTING - HANDS

If you brought brochures or paperwork about agencies and organizations that do compassion ministries, pass them around the group. Take time to read through the material to become educated and to explore the possibilities of getting involved. If you are able to narrow down your options, and you are ready to make a choice as an individual or as a group, share your decisions with the other in the group.

HEAD, HEART, HANDS & HABITS

Using the Gifts God Has Given You

EPHESIANS 4:11-13

INTRODUCTION

What's in your hand?

Moses had a staff. The little boy had two loaves and five fish. The widow had a coin.

Moses did miracles with his staff. The little boy's lunch fed thousands. The widow's offering brought Jesus' praise.

God doesn't ask you to be Moses or the little boy or widow. God wants you to be you.

Are you willing? God can do meaningful things through you. What's even more amazing is that He will do it with the gifts and talents *He gave you*. It's not about you but about God working through you.

Are you willing?

The introduction listed three people whom God used to do great things. Add to the list those that you remember from Scripture.

On a scale of 1–10, 1 being "not at all" and 10 being "very much," how much do you desire God to use you to accomplish His desires?

DISCOVERING TRUTH—HEAD

God has given each Christian spiritual gifts and talents that are to be used in the body of Christ. He graciously did not leave it up to chance for us to guess what our spiritual gifts are. He included lists in His Word, the Bible. The lists are not necessarily comprehensive, but include the most common ones that are used in a local church.

Have someone read 1 Corinthians 12:27–30, then 1 Corinthians 12:4–11. Discuss the facts that are given in

> How desperately we need to learn the basics of Christian stewardship! God owns everything; we own nothing. He places in our hands certain resources (time, talent, and treasures) that we are to use for His honor and glory in the building of His kingdom. What a privilege! What a responsibility!
>
> —Doug Carter, *Big Picture People*

explaining the origin and the purpose of the spiritual gifts. In addition, list the specific gifts that are found in these two passages.

Describe numerous ways how you have witnessed and experienced the spiritual gifts being practiced in your church.

Are there more contemporary labels that mean the same thing as what the Bible labels the gifts? For the sake of making greater application, list the gifts again using contemporary language.

Before people use their spiritual gifts, it is important to understand some of God's "ground rules." The Bible clearly emphasizes the purpose of the spiritual gifts as being for the "common good." It goes without saying that gifts have not or are not always used as such. Regardless, the Bible's mandate still stands. Spiritual gifts are not to be used for personal gratification or promotion. They are to be used for the good of all.

Turn to 1 Corinthians 12:7 again, and read it in unison. If you feel comfortable writing in your Bible, write your own first name just above the words "each one." Go around the circle and have each person reread the verse, inserting his or her own name.

Church leadership has historically taken the responsibility of "doing the ministry" as though it is their job. Church congregations have historically thought that it is, indeed, the job of the clergy to do God's work. However, as with many other topics, the Bible has something very revolutionary to say about such thinking

Have the leader of your group read Ephesians 4:11–13.

Compare this passage with the previous passages.

Discuss the key role of the leadership gifts—"to prepare God's people for works of service." How is this revolutionary? Does it challenge your mindset or confirm it?

To model this verse, and in the spirit of "preparing God's people for works of service," have the leader ask someone in the group to read Genesis 1:29–30. Again, have the

Therefore, I urge you, brothers, in view of God's mercy, to offer your bodies as living sacrifices, holy and pleasing to God—this is your spiritual act of worship. –Romans 12:1

leader ask someone to read Matthew 28:18–19. In these two passages God is also our example and Jesus is our example. Imagine how hard it must have been for God to create the world, say that it was good, and then hand over the responsibility of caring for the earth to Adam and Eve and their offspring. Imagine how hard it must have been for Jesus to invest, literally, His life into establishing the foundation for the church, and then hand it over to the disciples. If God and Jesus have asked us to carry on their work, would we decline to help carry on the work with our church leaders? Let this rhetorical question sink in by having one minute of silence.

EMBRACING TRUTH—HEART

God created us to serve. He gave us gifts and talents for the purpose of accomplishing His will for the world. It is important for each Christian to discover and clarify what spiritual gifts and talents he or she has. When we use our gifts and talents to bless others and ultimately serve God, we experience a deep, fulfilling joy. When we do not know our gifts and/or do not find a place to serve, we are not completing our purpose in life and do not experience the unique joy that accompanies serving.

Have each person silently read the parable of the talents in Matthew 25:14–30. Have a volunteer summarize the parable.

Why do you think that some people would not use their talents? Can you relate to any of these reasons? What do you think could be done to help people overcome these reasons?

Discuss the concept of "to whom much is given, much is required." Share how you feel about this concept, and include how you believe you are currently "measuring up" in regard to this important concept.

Read verse 21 again and describe a time when you experienced joy in using your spiritual gifts. Are you feeling joy in serving in some area now?

CONNECTING—HANDS

Give each person time to share how he or she may already be using their spiritual gifts and how their gifts build up the body of Christ. How do you prepare yourself to be in the right frame of mind as you enter your volunteer role? What are some of the negative attitudes that can tempt you to become discouraged complain or even quit? Be careful to make this a discussion about your own attitudes and not a time to complain about other people.

Break into groups of three or four. Have each person write a list of additional ways that God could use his or her spiritual gifts in the future. Share your list with the others in your group. Take turns choosing one thing from each list to give positive feedback to.

TAKE HOME—HABITS

What one point from the session do you want to remember to put into practice? What will you need to change or adjust to make sure that you follow through?

Is there a specific person in your church that you would like to encourage to use his or her spiritual gifts? Talk with your group how you can encourage that person without using guilt or coercion.

LOOKING FORWARD

We all need to be needed. God has created everyone with that longing to belong. Has your need been met? There is a place waiting for you—a place designed by God, especially with you in mind. In the next and final session you will find your place.

DIG DEEPER

1. Read Acts 20:35. Now, go back and read the apostle Paul's farewell in verses 13–38. Journal your observations concerning the great sacrifices Paul made as he served God. Take some time to journal your thoughts about your willingness to sacrifice.

2. Write Romans 12:1–2 on one side of an index card. On the other side, write some of the personal sacrifices that you make or will make to serve by using your spiritual gifts. Will your mind need to be transformed to make the sacrifices? If so, explain.

3. Read Matthew 25:14–30 in *The Message* or another modern translation.

DISCOVERING TRUTH - HEAD

Sometimes it is helpful when you know what others see in you. Take time to go around the circle and affirm (no negatives) each person and the spiritual gifts each person displays. Share a story or an example of when you have seen that spiritual gift in action. Be positive and encouraging.

EMBRACING TRUTH - HEART

Interview a couple people during the week and ask them if they are using their talents to benefit others. Ask further questions to discover more about them. For example, if they use their gifts, ask probing questions that can reveal their satisfaction or desire to do more. If they do not use their talents, ask questions such as "What do you think it would take for you to be able to use your talents to benefit others?"

CONNECTING - HANDS

Divide the group into partners and pray for God to confirm how that person is already serving or to guide him or her to a place (or additional place) to serve. Avoid the temptation to play God in people's lives for this exercise. Make it all about praying that God will guide the person.

HEAD, HEART, HANDS & HABITS

It's Time to Start

ROMANS 12:3-8

INTRODUCTION

This study has been for the purpose of finding that the Bible instructs us to serve for God's glory, our joy, and others' benefit. This study has not been intended to be a sales pitch to get you to help other people lighten their work loads. And, it has not been intended to give you a guilt trip. If you have never experienced the joy of serving, give it a try. If you sense God nudging you in a certain direction, follow Him. And, if you are serving, great! An important part of God's plan is happening because of you!

ICEBREAKER

Share what was gleaned from the previous "Digging Deeper."

What has been your most meaningful time of serving?

How have you grown through studying the topic of serving.

Role play a way you served this week. Have the others guess what it is.

DISCOVERING TRUTH—HEAD

It is all too common and very tempting to compare ourselves to each other. From talents to appearance to occupations to economic status, people feel inferior or superior according to comparisons. If we live by the Bible, we will not accept the status quo but will strive to find our worth in who God made us and the measure in which we are living out how He made us.

Read Romans 12:1–3. Allow time for each person to share the phrase or word that stood our most to him or her while this passage was being read.

Discuss the points of contrast in these verses.

The body of Christ is similar to a sports team. Each team member has a different position to play, but every player

> When we try to gratify this need for dignity through our fallen nature, we resort to pecking orders and politics . . . All this has to do with power and pride. We want to impress others (power) and we want to be impressed with ourselves (pride). But holiness, our thirst for dignity, is satisfied, oddly enough, through service.
>
> —Steve DeNeff, *More Than Forgiveness*

has the same goal—to win. The body of Christ is also similar to an orchestra. Each instrument has a different sound and different notes to play, but every musician in the orchestra has the same goal—to play beautiful music together.

To make this point, read Romans 12:4–8 by having each person in the group read one word while the next person reads the next word, and so forth, until the whole passage is read. It may take longer to read it, and it may be a little awkward or even confusing. But talk about the experience in an objective way by comparing it with the content of the passage.

Read 1 Corinthians 12:18–26. How does this passage reinforce Romans 12:1–8?

A local church family can often fall into the trap of subtly or not so subtly honoring certain spiritual gifts in the congregation over others. That is one reason why it is important to keep up your daily reading of the Bible. When you read the Bible daily, you are reminded of God's priorities and His ways.

Have the leader read 1 Corinthians 12:27–31. When the leader gets to the place where the passage asks rhetorical questions, have the rest of the group say no in unison after each question. Why is this point so important?

Notice that love is the topic of the next chapter. Define love in the context of a local church family.

Take time to read chapter 13. Discuss how chapters 12 and 13 complement each other. Explore the reasons why you suppose God arranged things this way.

Most people have experienced the opposite of love in the context of church or relationships. In fact, some of the most painful experiences that Christians have happen in the church. How sad it is when the place where the God of love asks us to remember and celebrate Him becomes the very place where we can do anything but celebrate. But, God's will is for us to live free from division, backbiting, gossip, hurtful actions and words, and all the other painful experiences that happen amongst us. Galatians 5:1 says, "It is for freedom that Christ has set us free."

As a group read, in unison, Galatians 5:13–15.

Discuss each verse, one at a time. How would you define the word *freedom* as a Christian? List some ways that

We serve God by serving others. The world defines greatness in terms of power, possessions, prestige, and position. If you can demand service from others, you've arrived. In our self-serving culture with its me-first mentality, acting like a servant is not a popular concept.

—Rick Warren, *Purpose Driven Life*

Christians "bite" and "devour" each other. Name some things on the list that you personally would like God to free you of.

EMBRACING TRUTH—HEART

You go to church this Sunday, and you meet the greeter at the door—an elderly woman who can barely stand upright. What thoughts about her do you have as you smile and receive her greeting? A single dad pushes past you, holding a little, disheveled boy, rushing to go upstairs to the children's programming before coming down to be an usher. How do you feel about him as you take the bulletin from his hand? The worship team sings with the quality of the CD in your car again this week. Their voices are perfect—and they are perfectly dressed! Is this when you start loving church, or did it start when you walked in the door?

We know better as Christians, but why are we tempted to compare people and their spiritual gifts? How do you feel about this?

Talk about the fact that when comparing people, we make one to be the "winner" and one to be the "loser." How do you feel this measures up to the 1 Corinthians 12 passage? How do you imagine the "winners" in a church feel? What are some of the advantages or disadvantages of being the "winners" in a church? How do you imagine the "losers" in a church feel? What are some of the disadvantages and advantages (if any) that the "losers" feel?

Have one or two people share a story of life experience when comparing people came into play.

If the group feels comfortable in doing so, share how each person feels they are treated as to their value in the local church. Be careful to keep this authentic, validating, and constructive.

CONNECTING—HANDS

Note a few people in your church who volunteer in a ministry and appear to be finding joy in serving. Consider asking them what led them to their place of serving.

Make a list of all the possible ways and places you would like to volunteer or serve in your lifetime. Include your local church, community, national, and international possibilities. Rank the list, starting with the opportunity you're most likely to get involved with now.

TAKE HOME—HABITS

Biblical truth is not useful until it is put into practice. It is stimulating to gain biblical knowledge. It is gratifying to discuss and analyze biblical truths. But until the biblical truth is put into practice and integrated into a Christian's life and lifestyle, it has not fulfilled its purpose.

Have the leader take some time to present ways of serving that are available in his or her local context—as well as larger community, national, or international opportunities for service.

As a group, gently hold each person accountable by asking if he or she is involved already or is committed to finding a place to serve.

Ask your pastor if there is any other way you could help in the church. If there is a lack of volunteers, ask if you can help to invite people to fill those roles.

DIG DEEPER

1. Keeping the topic of serving in mind, read through the Gospels and make note of Jesus' example. List the characteristics Jesus displayed as He served. For the next week as you read the Bible during your devotions, use this same thought process with the people in the passage, noting good examples as well as poor examples.

2. Read through the letters of Paul and make note of the many references to serving and using one's spiritual gifts.

3. Look in your Bible concordance for the first and last mention of *serve*. Analyze any significance that you find.

DISCOVERING TRUTH – HEAD

As a group or on your own time, further analyze the similarities and differences of the body of Christ with a sports team and orchestra. Which analogy do you relate to most? If your church were a sports team, would they be winning? If they were an orchestra, would people come to the concerts?

EMBRACING TRUTH – HEART

Discuss the following statement: "If everyone served where they sensed God to be leading, everything would get done."

CONNECTING - HANDS

As a group or individual, schedule an outing where you will be able to watch an athletic event or a concert. Afterward, take some time to discuss or journal your observations. In what ways can this inspire you to find your place in the body of Christ?

HEAD, HEART, HANDS & HABITS

NOTES:
HEAD, HEART, HANDS & HABITS

HEAD, HEART, HANDS & HABITS

NOTES:
HEAD, HEART, HANDS & HABITS

HEAD, HEART, HANDS & HABITS